C.B.

Eye, Thus Far, Unplucked

Eye, Thus Far, Unplucked

Collier Brown

Stephen F. Austin State University Press

2017

For more information:
Stephen F. Austin State University Press
P.O. Box 13007 SFA Station
Nacogdoches, Texas 75962
sfapress@sfasu.edu
www.sfasu.edu/sfapress

Distributed by Texas A&M Consortium
www.tamupress.com

ISBN: 978-1-62288-175-8

ACKNOWLEDGMENTS

"Demolition" *Terrain* (September 2016).

"A Friend's Dementia" *The Ocean State Review* (2016).

"The Small Bang" (now "The Limits") *The World Is Charged: Poetic Engagements with Gerard Manley Hopkins*, eds. Daniel Westover and William Wright (Clemson, SC: Clemson University Press, 2016).

"The Return" *The Freeman* (2015).

"Dirt Daubers" *Measure* 7.1 (2012).

"The Wingkeepers" *Poetry East* (2012).

"Real Estate" featured on *Verse Daily*, January 10, 2011.

"Penumbra" (now "Ordinance") *Best New Poets 2010*, selected by Claudia Emerson.

"Onward, Outward" (now "Nocturne") *Barrow Street*, Fall/Winter (2010).

"Real Estate," "Jar Season," and "Morning Auguries" (now "Atmospherics") *Unsplendid* 3.1 (2010).

"Conversions" (now "June Bugs & the Porch Man") *Asheville Poetry Review*, 19 (2009).

"June Interrupted" *Indiana Review* 31.1.

"Whale Bone" *Rattle* (2006).

for John Wood

CONTENTS

Preface

I first read Collier Brown's poetry in 2012. It spoke to me unlike any other poetry I've encountered before or since. I was editing the Louisiana volume of *The Southern Poetry Anthology*, and, understandably, many of the poems were about Louisiana life, landscape, and the perils of living in a state often upset by natural disaster. In Brown's poems, though, I noted a lyrical gift immediately, and perhaps most significantly, I recognized an imaginative force. In no way did I feel there were rhetorical or linguistic games being played to trick me, nor did I feel harassed by an agenda. And even though they evaded straight narrative, the poems were *packed* with stories.

Brown's poems unapologetically conflate the mystical with the modern, microcosm with macrocosm, the personal with the unknowable. It's almost eerie, really, how they create a language I wholly believe exists behind the language of the everyday. The poems do not merely tell me what I know unconsciously, they expand my consciousness through a stream of strangely coherent revelations.

Brown's work is textural and sonically charged. Take, for instance, an example from a poem entitled "Brother":

> The tree, dry
> as a jarred dragonfly.
> Mites and motelight choke
> in the shade. When I speak,
> it's to the fox teeth I gather
> near the creek. Brother,
> I say, show me your hand.
> Brother, he says, stand
> close to me. The slaughter
> is sure. Come taste this water.

The alliterative command, the neologistic "motelight," the stark contrasts between utterance and silence, the mysteries catalyzed by body, the aural lushness, and the nature-centric motifs run like distinct rivulets through the poem's creek. These qualities illuminate for me why the most important aspect of Brown's poetry is that it is a pleasure to read. That, to me, is successful poetry. And I am so very happy that a full-length volume of Brown's poetry is finally here.

—William Wright

WILLIAM WRIGHT is author of nine collections of poetry, most recently *Tree Heresies* (Mercer University Press, 2015). Wright serves as assistant editor for *Shenandoah* and is series editor of *The Southern Poetry Anthology*, a multivolume series celebrating contemporary writing of the American South, published by Texas Review Press. He is married to the writer, Michelle Wright

The Remedy

The Remedy

The sun's dull tusk
nudges at the bulk of fret
between my shoulder bones,

my wandering eye, thus far,
unplucked—a lucky thing.

A helicopter seed
descends discreetly down.

The city's power lines
spur the great ongoing failure,
and even with all that,
whisper sparrows to the air.

Perpetual Motion

The first thing is to tip it all
off balance. Fling it out
the window—wingback chairs,
pianos, prayers. Sunday let
the cloud's wreck come. The hail
to scuff spitshine off pines.
Catch the katydids awhile.
Or try. Or fail. Wring the clean
linen and lemon Ts and hang
each one on the line to sail.
If starlings swarm, swarm too.
There is no pattern, no equation.
Pat your belly, chew gum,
let the axis lean and tilt
a millimeter more and all
the dogs dash downhill
faster. If Maxwell's demon lets
you by, bless him with a dug-up
dime. The month of June will loan
itself to no day longer than
its last. It won't abide the boys
whose kickstands break, who can't
stop now, even though it's late
and long past time to go home.

Brother

Our catahoula hound
roams the unmowed ground
at every hour—makes hours
with its rounded tours,
buried to unburied kill.
A lizard on the windowsill
is a week dead. The tree, dry
as a jarred dragonfly.
Mites and motelight choke
in the shade. When I speak,
it's to the fox teeth I gather
near the creek. Brother,
I say, show me your hand.
Brother, he says, stand
close to me. The slaughter
is sure. Come taste this water.

Duck Tulip Ant

I'm liable not to cling
to a house burned down.
I'll not air my flat tire

or tie my shoes. It's spring
now. Only the known
shines, no shirt at all, all fire

in the fat bud. Undo black
ties. Scrape moon off
the bone. Bear no clutter.

The kids, after all, will kick
tulips into pulp, rough
the ducks with bad fodder.

It's their spring as well,
their race around the pond.
Six exquisite laps, three

to go, which can be hell:
violence, for sure, fraud,
treachery. Note the tree

here, the sap-clapped ant,
that other spring to come,
gold slumping lump, hot

to cold. Mr. Soon, I don't want
much, only the sweet time
it takes to get caught.

A Friend's Dementia

Icefalls spall an escarpment
off Mt. Monadnock. Glacial sap
slips and glints against the grit
gray matter of midday.
It's always midday, and you
amazed at ice, the hard rimed
larch, its lace links, a length
of the infinite winter branch.
But then, how easy the collapse,
astral in its way, at a gust
of almost nothing, a needle
loosed at the node, as we make
the drive we've often driven,
and you just as fresh to every
first impression, every view,
as a moment ago, and just enough
time for us to say so again.

Divinities

For 80,000 years, a colony of trees
near Richfield, Utah, has awed
the raw image of itself made over
by numerous, innumerable, facet eyes
of the pollinators as they dip.

There are some things that stand here
that shall not taste of death. They share
a root, a shamble of nucleotides,
a breath—the rest I describe, one
instant at a time, as to the sightless.

I stand for a bit on a tier of pine
and power lines, then walk on.
Birds align the circuitry, preen, twit,
then quit the view. They take away
their part. I let them have it, as a gift,
with twice a million lacewings.

The sun sets. The last awake things
dress dim depths of blue vetch.
They too see what I see, a stillness
so small, its walls are all we know:
the past a wall of stone, the future
a wall of snow, which is to say,
this instant may never truly exist.

I move to deeper grass. A black burr
afflicts my jeans. A June bug clicks.
There's nothing in myself I need
to last. I lend an eye to the blind
undying copse. It'll be here after I am
gone, with this brief sunset in its long
abysmal dream, to help its unbelief
in the perishing passers-by.

The Limits

I rub the Pentateuch away,
brush from the brainwall
the scientific law, to walk
once more against the limits.

The swallow-washed woods
are damage-dipped—days'
flit litter since nothingness
startled into weight and depth.

At dawn: an exodus of ants
will clasp at pips of sap.
At noon: the beetles tip
from sleep into the folioles.

At dusk: a darkness starts
its song. It says, go on, go on.
The frogs accord. A firefly
enraptured, claps me in its spark.

Voyager

Ordinance

A billion miles away
from a long gone Voyager 1,
our dogs lap spores from off
the year's hot drinking holes.

Wet light and water wince
like silkworms in the trees.
The evening rests its injured
elbows. Or the mayflies blow
whichever way—beneath
the sidewalk kliegs, or else
like gods in the dogs' mouths.

Water deepens every
ordinance of dirt,
every high-and-dry.

therefore

the daughters of this world
spit dimes into their flowerpots

where rings on rings rinse
orbital, with rhythms of
inconsequence, except
that each new ring begins
its welcome to the ends.

And near the porchbulbshine,
the sons reach out to touch
thin flutters of dust,
not so very far
from the bones within their hands.

The Shaper

Rain grates. The cockroach grows
by eons weaved in wet wood.
The power lines in two neat rows
hold gold older than the mud.

I keep a chestnut in a jar.
Behind my ear I keep a dime.
I've made arrangements with a star
to meet me in the bone sometime.

Clip clup, I've bagged my cabbage up
and kept my secrets high and dry.
I've loved this cracked ugly cup.
Breath by breath I've shaped the sky.

Arrival

Time now for the day to hang
long. Sunset licks the last cocoon,
the flit of goldfinch and festoon
of paper dolls my daughters hung.

Far off, the satellites will merge
with silage and the lightning germ
above the gulf. It's time for storm
and the blue luciferin surge.

Mudchrist of the murder south
undo your fist and be fulfilled.
Keep us from the darkness rolled
tight in the butterfly's mouth.

Our More Furious Selves

A jackdaw jots the blistered lawn.
The earth heaps white heat
and spreads it out like wheat.
Only wing-born bear the sun

and levitate. I can't pretend
otherwise—wish the bloodmeal
in me gone. My solace is the real
fire, the far star's singe. I bend

to give the bird what small regret
I hold—a naked stick he picks
until he's furious. His neck's
wretched as a cigarette.

I let him go, don't urge again
the little wraths I love to love
so much, like cursing at the stove
or the snow ahead, or the sin

of this foregone appetite
for wasting time. It's in his face—
he'll have no fight, abide no fuss.
He'll gather gift, leaping light.

Dog Star

When plan failed,
when house burned,
when leader lied,
when money went,
when health turned,
when sick spread,
when bread dried,

no dogs died
or whales bled,
no trees fled,
no rock stirred.

No dirt's seed,
no light's speed
its share spared.

The Sweetness

It came, as it does, on Sunday.
We boys sat satchel slack on a bench
beneath blue windowpanes of bearded
women soldered to the wheatlight
of June, draped with jam. Somehow
in long Southern drawls they sang
In the Sweet By and By, and the blood
was like the sweet scuppernong
licked sideways off a scythe.

I saw, to the east of that first tryst,
the season's crisp cut sugarcane
burned to bitter shards. The wind
caught the scent of it, baptismal,
and bathed the aisles, the soaped faces.
From an open door, I noticed how
a stripped sycamore, bare enough
to climb, opened up its arms.

There'd be no flood, no last fire.
The gospel of that fact, the glare
beyond stained glass, the blood
I tried to rinse but never could
stole from me the stillness, the need
to be held rapt. I'd run to the mud
eventually, dip myself and stand,
my branches wide beneath light,
made in the image of each instant
and no other.

Portrait after Radiation Treatment

The waiting room has twelve cold seats.
The vinyl floor divides itself by white.
They make me wait here, where
the sense of smell and touch go blind.

A coke can drops from a machine in
outer space. When I return, you're asleep
but haven't closed your eyes. Night
makes the window paint your face.

In 1878, the German Wilhelm Kühne
fixed the last thing his rabbit saw
onto its retina, strange polaroid. It showed
a dormer. There were seven panes.
Six were square, one was like a moon.

Whale Bone

Most days, the wind is too far off
like a fish to the Negev,

and finally I think
the summer will not go.

But then, as if it knew
my days on earth
were unpredictable as lightning path,

as if it knew that for love to work
it must catch up, it must travel fast,

it breaks the balustrade,
blows away the snug serene,
its heavy bones milled and cast.

Here, the whales go by,
all breath,
touching things that cannot last.

Once Giants

Sons of Anak,
or Recollections of a Summer River

Before the dream of man,
we never wore our shoes

grew needles of a gar's glass teeth.
we leapt in floods headfirst

Egrets slipped their necks
we struck a million matchsticks

into the pain of sharp palmetto.
we outbled each other fair

But then, the nephilim in fur
we bit our knives in the bark

walked off into the fogs,
we grew up, had to leave

their story never understood
we speak like fire in the bogs

a story that began: Once, giants
we

The Fourth

The gulls pinwheel above debris.
The dead assemble in their shells.

Insect skylines click, *click click.*
Another year beneath the pier.

Kids with sparklers scrape their age
against the night to fix themselves

in light—each firework a wish beneath
the eyeless dark-toothed fish.

Jar Season

It comes suddenly, in chorus,
those moments of solarium,
the Junes that nursed and kept us
sons and daughters of the field,
or slept us on the beaming slew
of moonlight—interminable shield
against the wash of wasted hours,
taste of dry oat and sassafras tea,
the bitter leaf of failure's flower.

Stars out, how often I'd recline
in the plant-dismantled Plymouth
smiled over with muscadine,
beside the honeycombs that spread
throughout our western wall.
I filled jars where the house bled.

Now wasps pack up those holes
with mud. The shutters' wood
recedes back down into the boles,
the bread back down to the grain.
And nowhere a rebirth. Some burst
of lyric may flutter, but in a brain
finally to be crushed by wonder.

Sometimes those June mantras
boom inside my ear like thunder
beneath an oak, where once a kiss
left teeth marks in my bottom lip.
What we aimed for became a miss
that bled and brightened tight—
a wall my head hit (still hits), caught
as I was, off guard, and in flight.

Latchkey Lessons

The bus lugs away
as if the distance
from street to door
were not worth waiting for.

Home again, or at least,
the house that takes his key.

The neighbors say to one another
Lord, Lord. But the Lord
giveth him the wheel.

He oils his bike chain
and polishes the seat
to a beetle-slick sheen.

He shows up at the woods
with a small regime of dogs
and a stolen magazine
with hints of trimmed hair
that climb and glisten
like nothing in the naked air.

The other boys add their twos
and fives, fill their brains
with the capitals of Idaho and Maine.
What else is there to learn?

Piles of appliances
lie waiting to be burned.
Behind the house
he builds the boxspring fire.

Lord, Lord
your boy plays the buckets proud.
He dances on the mattress wire.

Wingkeepers

The boys scud a length of lawn,
jars full of bees, a digging pail—

in it, a wreath of beetle wings,
good dung kicked loose,
sunlight's luminous breads,
the rain with its thousand meals.

More hours than the day can lose,
they go and go and go—despite

fence barbs and felled branch,
the stones that nick the skin,
despite the nests of pretty bones.

In the end, they say the just leave
and gather to a golden world.
But praise be to the boys of the field
who will not make it far from here.

Wormlight

At seven, I stopped
sleeping outside. God
fell, Its belly flecked
with fields of wormlight.

I heard Its hum,
gumming like an infant
on the rusted roof.

My parents slept below,
nuzzled in June's oven,
dreaming their meaty dreams.

And the river, rheumy
as a kid's sick eye,
watched them sleep
and would not flow.

An owl gagged
on something hatched.
A green anole
grew lovely in the throat
and struck its skull
against the windowpane

as if to say, *No one sleeps,*
no one sleeps
and no one dreams entirely

which is the law
of worms weaving
lightning in the dark,

and all those born
beneath the open claw.

Ascensions

They've taken oaths to other worlds:
those who bite blind vipers,
saucer-seers, abductees,
the ones who've cut their wordlists down
to "End" and "Now." I think of them
at times like this—my chair drawn close
to open doors, near untold sums
of birds who turn like the turn of a whale.
I see my nine-year-old outside.
She's found a lilac freckled egg
beneath a hutch of hair and floss.
She pockets it without a thought
to what it all portends: the patterned
bluebirds on her dress that brush
against the blessed nevertheless
of every atom in the air.

Nectarines

Christ was crating oranges
when the violets hit.

Winter's roof and shutters
whipped from off the slab
and the mayhaw stripped itself
down to a dangling root.

It was late March,
with its floral maelstroms,
charged with primal recitation.

The children, two-to-three
on a bike's blue handlebar,
clamored their kazoos,
pelting open air
with lip-red nectarines

while fathers whispered
unintelligibly
into little dirt holes,
then kicked in dirt behind

as if something more than fruit
would grow,
some other place and time.

Real Estate

Real Estate

We moved the trailer to a lot
and bought a pull-crank mower.
We had a daughter there. I got
a fix-it book and slept an hour

when I could. I kept the buckets
full of tar against the April
ants. I polished copper faucets
and the floors of our cathedral.

We were carpenters, a guild
of two. We prayed with wood
like solitary gods. We built
and thought the building good.

We forgot about the universe
and saved for the long haul,
vacation time, an empty purse,
the day when accident would call,

a hurricane, a wreck, or theft.

It came.

       I found a few dead bees
on the casement when you left.
The bodies lifted in the breeze.

Each box we could not sell or keep,
I took out to the road. A wren
I used to feed fell in his sleep,
and bees gathered on the garbage men.

Nocturne

Sometimes the moon
rakes the kennel clean
and dogs turn orchids
about the howling mouth.

I balance down the hall
on a single thread of motion,
past windows masked with moths
and photographs of children,

their playthings perched
like grackles on their hats
to lift them, fully fledged,
for the onward, outward

flight. The mouth says:
It is difficult, boy. Out there,
it is difficult. But that part of me
that slings and will not sleep

undresses on the roof,
while dogs dig down
and out of themselves,
and the moon says *death*

is but the bone's light awake,
walking thin thread between
the moths and carpal stars.

Dirt Daubers

Armadillos dig beneath
the porch of Mr. Derelict.

The termites work through
lunch. A ventilation duct

appears, then ten. They etch
their amours into my bed.

Outside, not a fly in sight.
Inside, they're never dead.

Which is why I let the ants
excoriate the paint

and woodworms sculpt
their sacrificial saint.

For every patrolling roach
I leave the apple core.

Again, I spend the afternoon
sealing roof and floor.

The wasp inspects that too,
certain of the damage I can do.

Demolition

Perforate the curtains and the roof,
amplify the kettle till the bulb
breaks, disassemble, brick by brick,
the egg yolk yellow sitting room
if that will let the stars in, the rain,
the pollens that perfume blonde bees—
whatever it is that piques, greens,
plumes and makes the home no place
to live for the living, whatever it is
that makes inside a disgrace, where
even outside is barely enough space
for the eyes of one body to exist.

Trespass

After the week-long rains
the mice move their loose
militias to mobile homes.

But they avoid the traps,
the poison logs, to die
in the walls. They smell
of curds and turned eggs.
It's their way of staying.

If we pry the paneling
off the frame, what a spill
of bone, of brittle relics,
of spine like prayer beads
fit for an infant's wrist.

At night, we listen close
to matchstick-scratching
behind the lamp, above
the armoire. If it is prayer,
it is against the likes of us,
our soap and cold milk,
the white rose in a vase—
a familiar prayer: to get
inside, to get their way.

Aversions

Avoiding rooms where cold
and cracks in happiness collect,

I drag a chair up to the stove,
open up the oven just a hair

and close the doors against
the nightly flit of anti-collision lights.

For now, the Far Off fails
to nudge me into nothing.

The planes will do for stars.
My elbows dull their sharp degrees.

A branch behind the blinds
annuls its nightly avalanche.

The Clothesline

The trick is to let the dirt
do what it will do, just sift,
while katydid, fescue, star
slow across the linen drift.

Tracks

When you were here, we
watched the juncos snatch
at bramblebirth, then scatter out
and back. In a ditch, a mat
of fuzz would fascinate
a swarm. The calicos would itch
at cartilage, claw to wake it up
with expectation. I saw it
in the grin of fence wire,
even the leaf scars. That life
is not so far from me now,
like a season, red leaf, a snow.
We found a rabbit on those tracks,
remember? Later in the year,
we loved the bones together.
For a long time, I went back.

Alien Star

June Bugs & the Porch Man

—a remembrance of my grandfather

Not given to dreams, he drew smoke
and jawed on wads of comb white wax
right up to the end. Even as my cousins
conjured Christ beside his bed, he saw
the dragonflies glint in clean water.

Outside, red pears heaped on limbs.
Bees seamed numericals of eight
above a flower's fingertips. Wind bent
the purple sugarcane. They prayed
through dusk, while the beetle dug
deep, too deep to mean much
to the white bird's inscrutable clutch.

The Bean Psalm

The peonies swell in an opal vase,
the tabletop's cleared of catalogues.
Our underthings clothe the spectral race.
Constellations mark the godding spawn,
while crickets love like lions on the lawn.

Apocrypha

In the last days, the June dogs
will gnaw jaw bones
in cramped cars. The red
rear lights will mix into the white
and stall like orchard stillness
in a pink Spring.
If the angels see the dead,
they'll play their brass a bit,
and one will have to kiss
the pale horse on the brain
and comb its worried tail.

Imagine then the open fields,
open to the winged things,
no more horns to blow,
wheeling toward the wheat below,
exempt from god's largesse—
ten thousand virgins,
gilded streets, the golden vine—
now that it has come, their time
to beseech the leaves again
at the right hands of the trees.

The Signs

Cotton spot in the eye, moth in each knee,
bird inside my chest. One more blackout
for the books. Twice last month, twice in June

I stopped, to become, if only minutes at a time,
less than the no-place we traveled from, plus
the time it took to get here, plus accident, plus chance.

I start to write what can't be said. Therefore
I tie my feet against a pine, brace myself
for what came before myself, before I stood
and fell   from a crib of star and wood.

Era Vulgaris

—after Theo Jansen's "Stranbeest"

On the beach, we bucket twine and PVC,
empty bottles of lemonade, the rind
of a flip flop—what you'd expect to find
in a place where each year the sea
unravels to a nakedness of netted krill,
a pink carapace for my windowsill.

If anything, the joggers-by just log
in their pedometers the steps they take
to dodge the mess. Or if, for the sake
of his good conscience, my analog
should say, *I try, I do, I don't pretend
or look away*, then it's only the end.

At least, that's what he means by *try*.
And anyway, the end was bound to come.
No rough beast, no second Bethlehem,
just little demonstrations of the octopi
inside their jars—another talent to ignore,
while wreckage walks onto the shore.

The Lizard & Loie Fuller

A lizard on the window
parodies split figs. A mirage
in cement repeats in pink florets
a phrase of saxifrage.

The day loves Loie Fuller.
The sprinkler swings
its dress above the dogs
who snip at glitzy underthings.

Millions of dimes will not do,
none of that rococo trouble
because this, the penniless
world made double,

is what we want—our wish
to leave the bone's Y
unbroken. A reflection in the glass
licks a planetary eye.

Three Views of the Night Sky

I. From the Ground

Mothered by mudslide,
here we are at last—we
laughing, weeping animals,
and the fatal optometry

that Empedocles said
turns the eye into a flint
so that whatever I see,
no matter how innocent

my wish upon my star,
my star reflects much faster
only us, as we are to it—
what already was disaster.

II. From the Tree

The street lamps at half past ten,
like magicians with serviettes,
show glyphics of a jogger's sweats.
I should see (a clear night like this)
Orion's belt, the Alkaid of the Bear
and Dipper. Instead, Delta Air
dots a starless arc. On Trapelo Road,
the beech's ailing elephant skin
is scrawled with Sanskrit and broken
hearts—my daughter's climbing tree.
The apes, I tell her, once sang
to stars. She says she knows the song.
The blinking jets are such a bore.
She's waiting for the final flight
to have it to herself, the diamond night.

III. From the Road

That abandoned, ruined
Buick stranded in East Texas
is no accident—no glass
smashed or brake fluid.

The field beyond traffic
lanes, that's sugarcane, as far
as far can go. That gray hair
on the sky's ridge, that's brisk

unexpected rain. That void
between Dog Star and cloud,
8.6 light years from plowed
fields, that's outside of outside

where Flammarion lost his head
in the circuitry of first fire.
In the glass, I see myself, but higher,
in a bright braid of giants dead.

Earth upon Earth

Earth upon Earth

The earth earth enough? she asks.
the tree tree enough, the stuff
of stars enough? If she risks
listening to beetles in the rough
reeds sing, she may not find
disaster after all, or the reprimand

one expects, at times, just for being
alive (good luck's weak arrow
so likely to miss). She'll have to wring
her hands another day. For now,
she's worriless beneath a whirligig
of winged seeds. And she will dig,

shortly, if the moment survives,
in the red dirt—until she reaches
stones with fossil afterlives.
She will see in their relic niches
eyes that were not eyes, just spots.
But in their lobes begins and stops

a first impression: a life not quite
life without the sun flaked on lake-
dusk, the oak in its sparrow coat,
the night's incessant natal ache
and, she sees it now, her connection
to every earth, enough perfection.

The Avid

The waxwing boys still lose their hats
in the sun. The birds and fisher cats
finish off the bones. The cell phone
chirrups trouble, but the black stone
I found on Friday has a twin for me
in the river. The million myths we
made are true and untrue. I can't tell
(no one can) the lab's synthetic cell
from any other. Maybe we will live
forever now. Maybe we'll make love
to trees. True hell is just a solar flare.
It doesn't change the view from here.

Wide eye, delight me as you did at ten,
or don't. Either way, let the day begin.

Boondoggle

In the glee roulade
of loud tree frogs,
the swat of hot rain
running puddles up
the sun, June bugs
crack the catafalque
of dusk, crickets
cast black reticules.

What was fishing line
and orange cork
dangles from the dead
tree limbs—lanyards
of a missed intent,
many of them mine,
except once made
they catch blue glass,
bottle caps, bright tin,
beginning gifts
for no good reason.

Courage

I sprawl south, east, and west
in kindergartens of perking crocus.
The robins chase a chandelier
of light across the small moss
bluffs. I chase a few dead cells
behind my eyes, like broken oak
washed sideways on the waves.
2,000 years ago, holy men ate
locusts in the wild to get to this
place. In another 2,000 years,
that might be true again. Surely,
it's in the hieroglyphs or high
dry caves, that bit of evidence
that shows the other man, afloat
on his back, singing *cuc cu nu*,
never there for the 2AM attack.

Atmospherics

It's fortunate that we've woken
early. The neighbor's dog is underneath
the shed asleep. The mower's broken
blade is still broken, the finch's bath
full of leaf trash, the street as well.
Morning ends the long night's flood—
for now, for us. Miracles are hard to sell.
The sun scatters pennies on the mud.

Calcasieu Sacristy

Late bugs turn their ratchet mouths
around the sun, grinding light
like strings of meat
and mucked into the summer's gut.

The pollywogs walk on water,
praise be. The mud, sing brother, sings.
I slick my hair to spawn shine
and hundreds of beginnings.

June Interrupted

The birds whose bones
abridge the sun and dirt,
whose brains sip wind,
spill prophetic chatter
over fountains full of coins
and the sweet unspeakable wish.

But I (that impossible word)
wreck the wish with praise
for teal ten-thousand-winged,
for the golden meaningless days.

Notes

"Perpetual Motion"
Maxwell's demon is a thought experiment designed by James Clerk Maxwell. In the experiment, a demon opens and closes a small door between two gas chambers. The demon lets fast, hot molecules pass into one room while the slow, cool molecules stay trapped in the other. Of course, this violates the second law of thermodynamics that says matter, or energy, degrades and cools. Maxwell's demon thwarts entropy.

"Duck Tulip Ant"
The title is a play on *Ente, Tod, und Tulpe* (Duck, Death, and Tulip), a popular German children's book by Wolf Elbruch.

"Violence," "Fraud," and "Treachery," refer to the last three circles (out of nine) of hell in Dante's *Inferno*.

"Divinities"
The 80,000-year-old grove of quaking aspen, Pando, is connected by a single root system and is among the oldest living organisms on this planet.

"The Sons of Anak"
In the Old Testament's Book of Numbers, Anak was said to be the forefather of giants called Anakim. These giants were thought to be descended from nephilim, a mixed race of men with human mothers and angel fathers.

"Era Vulgaris" (Common Era)
Theo Jansen is the inventor of the Strandbeest, an "animal" made of plastic tubes and plastic bottles that walks on the beaches, harnessing the wind for fuel and self-propelled. "Since 1990," says Jansen, "I have been occupied creating new forms of life. Not pollen or seeds but plastic yellow tubes are used as the basic material of this new nature. I make skeletons that are able to walk on the wind, so they don't have to eat. Over time, these skeletons

have become increasingly better at surviving the elements such as storm and water and eventually I want to put these animals out in herds on the beaches, so they will live their own lives."

"Three Views of the Night Sky"
The pre-Socratic philosopher, Empedocles (c. 490 – c. 430 BCE), believed that the human eye emits light and that Aphrodite sparked the eye's initial fire.

Camille Flammarion (26 February 1842 – 3 June 1925) was an influential French author and astronomer after whose work, *L'atmosphère: métérologie populaire* (1888), a now-famous etching was created, the artist of which is unknown. In the etching, Flammarion pokes his head outside the celestial sphere.

The Stelliferous Era is the second of the five ages of the universe, and it is the age in which we live now. The end of this era will mean the end of the bright stars.

"Earth upon Earth"
"Erthe upon Erthe" was a popular Middle English poem usually inscribed on the blank pages at the start or ending of a book. It was a *memento mori*, reminding the reader of his or her transience. The word "earth" repeats and is used in a religious context, the first "earth" depicting man as dust and the second "earth" as the world. Many versions of the poem exist, and it appeared frequently up to the nineteenth century, inscribed on tombstones. See Hilda Murray, *Erthe upon Erthe* (1911; London: Oxford University Press, 1964).

Sample stanza:
Erth owte of erth is wondyrly wroght,
Ffor erth hath geten of erth a nobul thyng of noght,
Erthe uppon erthe hath set alle hys thoght
How erthe uppon erthe may be hygh broght.

"Courage"
"cu cu nu" is a wacky refrain from the famous medieval poem,
"Sumer Is Icumen In."

"Courage" at "2 AM": paraphrase of famous line by Napoleon:
"As to moral courage, I have very rarely met with the two o'clock
in the morning kind: I mean unprepared courage."